KEEPING THE
COLOURS NEW

First published 2003 at W&G Baird Ltd., Antrim on
behalf of Shalom House Poetry Group, c/o Ruth Carr,
BIFHE, Dunlewey Centre, 1a Dunlewey Street,
Belfast BT13 2QU

ISBN: 1 870157 49 4

Printed and bound by W&G Baird Ltd.

The cover and inserts are from an original textile
artwork by Lorsha Design, Buttercrane Centre, Newry.
Copyright for this work has been secured by Shalom
Poetry Group for this anthology but remains with
Lorsha Design.

This anthology has been funded through the support of
the 'Awards for All' scheme administered by the Arts
Council of Northern Ireland.

AWARDS
FOR ALL

KEEPING THE COLOURS NEW

**An anthology of poetry
by Shalom House Poetry Group**

editors

Lindsay Hodges, Alastair Browne, Vivien Paton

Acknowledgments

Shalom House Poetry Group gratefully acknowledges
the 'Awards for All' scheme and the Arts Council for
Northern Ireland for their generous funding and
support of this publication.

Thanks are also due to the Belfast Institute of Further
and Higher Education (BIFHE) and the Shalom House
Centre, Cliftonville Road, Belfast.

The Group would also like to thank Eddie Briggs and
the staff of W&G Baird Ltd printers for advice,
assistance and excellent production of this book.

Some of the poets featured in this anthology have
previously had work published in *The Lonely Poets' Guide
to Belfast*, *Fortnight Magazine*, *The Irish News*, *Poetry
Ireland*, *Omnibus*, *The Honest Ulsterman*, *Gown*, *The
Belfast Telegraph*, *Alchemy*, *The Sunday Tribune* and
Women's News.

Finally, all members of Shalom House Poetry Group
wish to thank Ruth Carr for her expertise as tutor and
poet, together with her invaluable encouragement,
enthusiasm and inspiration.

Contents

"This, you implied, is how we ought to live -

The ironical, loving crush of roses against snow,
Each fragile, solving ambiguity. So
From the pneumonia of the ditch, from the ague
Of the blind poet and the bombed-out town you bring
The all-clear to the empty holes of spring,
Rinsing the choked mud, keeping the colours new."

Derek Mahon

'In Carrowdore Churchyard (at the grave of Louis MacNeice)'

Foreword

In September of 2001 a new poetry class was offered by the Belfast Institute of Further & Higher Education. It differed from others I had taken, in that it was intended for individuals who were already committed to poetry and were seeking a critical forum for their work. The idea was that the class would provide a friendly but rigorous first audience for poems which would hopefully benefit as a result, and ultimately reach a wider audience through publication.

The class took a while to establish numbers. Yet even in the early stages, I could tell that something exciting was happening. There was a real buzz as each poem was read closely and discussed. Creative engagement with poetic craft was taking place. By the second year the class had grown and the work was developing steadily and getting published. The poetry was flowing and the format was working. The idea of putting together an anthology seemed right.

Some say that if you join a group your writing can become derivative and indistinguishable from that of other members. My experience suggests it works the other way, and that far from being compromised by the collective critical process, work is sharpened and made all the more credibly distinct for it. The voices rising from this anthology are certainly distinct – as different from one another as the authors themselves.

To give an indication of the rich diversity of style and theme addressed in this anthology, I have plucked out just a few of my favourite lines. I love Alastair Browne's response to Rilke's Elegies, as he contemplates our ironic reluctance to let go of this world, this "geography for pain", and our assumed importance in others' lives –

> What will become of them
> Without the protective blanket of our care?
> Hard to be reconciled.

> Aware, this ability is by ourselves, absurdly overrated,

> *(Hang Back)*

In direct contrast, Vivien Paton bravely faces, on her mother's death, the bleak fact that

    We missed each other all our lives.   *(Poems For My Parents)*

rendered all the more telling by the spareness of form and language.

If you thought you knew all there was to the mood of blue, read Lindsay Hodges' beautiful meditation on "the hue of longing".

    as if I'd slit
    the slender skin of water,
    slipped under,
    found the subtle tone of irises   *(Blue Beyond Midnight)*

But don't stop there, as Tom Honey has another blue to add –

    Gathered in drifts beneath the trees
    we find the truant sky.   *(Bluebells)*

Bluebells will forever more reflect that "truant sky" for me.

Childhood is a strong theme in Pat Taylor's and Maura Rea's poetry. Pat evokes a sense of time and place so vividly you can imagine yourself there –

    Entering the cool Plantin
    I drink from a spring
    that has already spoiled me
    for any other water.   *(By The River)*

While, in several poems, Maura brings home, with simple yet complex directness the utter isolation of a child abused –

> I don't want
> to love him
> but mummy says
> I have to
> and my teacher
> says God says
> I have to.   *(Brotherly Love)*

Many a person is celebrated within this anthology, but in Denis O'Sulivan's *Eulogy For A Fisherman* the art of meditation is celebrated through the portrayal of one who "wears his feathers/ like a crown of thorns" –

> The spreading ripples
> wrap him up in peace
> that is the core of self and self the core.

It is always refreshing to get another take on things, to see things anew. A number of poems in the book address things from an unusual angle. None more so than in Catherine Leslie's original outlook -

> I ate your limp today
> from the allotted
> space on my plate,   *(A4)*

Equally thought provoking is Noreen Campbell's quirky little masterpiece, *Ode To A Potato,* which she wrote while waiting at a bus stop. Would that all waiting for buses could be so inspirational!

> You lie cradled in my hand,
> Your creamy skin touching mine,
> Sightless eyes wide open.
>
> The hand in which you lie
> Can show no mercy,
> As hunger is pitiless.

This book could not have happened without the input and individual expertise of members of the group. The whole enterprise, from the initial raising of funds to the proofing of the last page – and the agreed giveaway price of less than a fiver – is the result of their combined efforts. I cannot think of a more fitting title for it than the one they have chosen themselves – *Keeping The Colours New,* taken from Derek Mahon's marvellous tribute to Louis MacNeice. There is no sounder example of poetry and its vast possibilities to encompass and articulate the human spirit than that left to us by Louis MacNeice. The title suggests to me that poetry is an active commitment to hold to the creative spark despite everything that would dull and diminish that aspiration. I heartily commend this anthology to all who open its pages, and raise a glass to the poets, whose endeavours do indeed live up to their aim of *Keeping The Colours New.*

Ruth Carr, November, 2003

ALASTAIR BROWNE

Alastair Browne lives in Belfast and is married with two daughters.

After graduating with a First in English, and completing an MA (mostly nineteenth century poetry), he qualified as a chartered accountant, became a partner in a major UK practice and latterly ran his own management consultancy business.

Gradually, poetry reasserted its importance. These are the first poems he has published.

STANDING WATER

Into the well of my undoing,
Falls, ripely, an overhanging plum,
Which I've been watching all through summer:

Wishing it would come.

BAUCIS AND PHILEMON

These very modest expectations for a life
Consist in the very happiness of being left alone,
Not being noticed,
Not being of any interest,
Not falling, inadvertently, into the path of great events,
Having enough, nothing to excess,
Shielded from the superfluous:
Envy, ambition, arrogance and lust,
Just,
This succession of shared ordinary days,
Days not taken for granted, received in trust,
Gratefully and carefully expended.

These larger things the foolish strive for,
We till the soil, and know as dust.

HANG BACK

As one might halt upon the last high ground,
Which shows him his own valley one last time
And turn; and linger; and hang back.

Rilke: *Duino Elegies 8*

What is it that we say goodbye to after all?
The world, ourselves, our friends,
Our unaccomplished effort,
Those we have loved
Their unknowable futures?

Turning back to gaze down that enclosed valley,
Slag heaps of spent workings,
Rain and grime;
The leavings of a more productive time,
The dereliction of a way of life, abandoned.

There must be some pleasure in letting all this go,
The ice field that gouged it out
Will no doubt come again,
Create a brand new language for this earth,
Provide a fresh geography for pain.

But oh, in the meantime,
The unknowable immediate futures of those we have loved,
What will become of them,
Without the protective blanket of our care?
Hard to be reconciled.

Aware, this ability is by ourselves, absurdly overrated,
Things will turn out, as always, much as they are fated.

BLUFF

My seventeen year-old,
Has just pronounced the dialogue in *Rigoletto,*
Profoundly banal!

This, straight out of the blue,
As I'm dumbing down to some amusing TV show.
Taken up short,
Desperately searching for the appropriate retort,
Knowing it's time to bluff.

Witter lamely about libretti,
Recitative,
(Out of my depth, already)
Wonder where the little rat has got this from,
Ridiculously narked the presumption of my superior knowledge,
Has taken yet another knock.

Gazing at her darkly,
Planning operatic revenge.

DURER'S HANDS

This is how it works:

I'm in my mother's room.
I sit on the bed,
She sits on the chair.

Right in front of me
Is the wardrobe mirror,
Impossible not to look;
She talks incoherently, I half listen,
Cross and re-cross my legs,
Find myself examining my hands,
Linking them
Backhand, forehand, sideways,
Like two undisciplined rugby packs
Binding restlessly, uneasily, unsuccessfully
Together.

They don't go palm to palm,
They don't form the prayer steeple,
Nothing any longer to be looked for
Beyond themselves.

IDYLL

Back then, sometime,
On a stopping train near Naples,
Third class, wooden slatted seats,
Window down, hot breeze in our faces,
The smell of high scorching, seeding summer,
Dust and masked fragrances,
Golden corn fields,
(Could there really have been all of these?)
Far endless avenues of trees,
Rattling down an idyll
Of our quite separate experiencing,
Away from everything,
Immersed in that moment,
Sailing through happiness
Under cloudless skies.

TIRTHA

That crossing space,
Threshold,
Revelation,
Where the sacred, timeless,
Becomes immanent,
Penetrates the sordid and mundane,
Redeems it,
Where the two become one
And the sinner transported is briefly with God,
In a reverent state of grace:

Life's irrelevancies fall away
In transfixed absorption in His face,
His welcoming embrace.

Surcease.

CHRISTIE'S SOAP FACTORY

Thirteen.
Your first job.
You sit on a bike machine all day
Pedalling.
Knives instead of a front wheel.

They put the soap blocks
Hot from the vat
In front of you.
You pedal, knives flay,
A soap-flake blizzard at the height of summer.
Sweat.

Sunlight from shaded windows
Slants,
Your pants wet, legs sore,
Eyes watering from dust.
Surely life must have more, much more
To offer
You, fresh from the open shores of childhood.

CATCHIES

Over all this distance,
I can still see their flickering, moony faces,
Reflecting the evening sun,
Half hidden behind the thorn hedge,
Striving to be inconspicuous.

I'm on.
They're looking for an opportunity to duke past,
Across the road to the telegraph pole:
Home.

There's no traffic
So you can run blind.
I'm moving left and right
Covering all the angles,
But then, Elizabeth, she's always the one,
Is gone.

I hear her whoop of triumph from over my shoulder,
And imagine this is what adults mean by love.

NEGEV

Apparently they did find human remains
In the excavated rubble of this defensive hill settlement,
Occupied, they guess, about 5000 years ago.

It's very hot.
It's been an arduous climb to get here,
Up from the long dead sea I'm gazing over.

Just the day before yesterday.

Seeds and grains,
Animal bones,
Some evidence of ritualistic activity,
(Though this remains a matter of dispute in the journals)
Provide a schemata of life as it was lived.

Just the day before yesterday.

A little boy chases his sister
Into tomorrow,
They are gloriously dirty and laughing:
Their mother chides.

They pause for a moment,
Look through me as if I wasn't there,
Continue with the game.

FRAGONARD AT THE VILLA D'ESTE: 1760

Much as it is today,
An artificial garden taken out of time,
Elaborate hydraulics driving streams and fountains,
Nooks, crannies, covered walks,
You can hardly imagine that beyond the high screening wall
Lies all the confusion, bustle of a busy town.

As an afterthought, he's added some rustic figures,
To romanticise the scene in current fashion, picturesque:
A little boy with a wheelbarrow,
A boy and girl seated on the steps,
In this easygoing gouache study.

When we first visited,
All those years ago
On our first foreign foray together,
Smitten.
It wouldn't have been difficult at all
To see it as a féte champétre, courtly love tableau,
(Perhaps an arbour swing, some glimmering silk, a parasol?).
We seemed to stay for hours,
Ate a lunch of oranges and dry bread,
Some place of shade.

Coming back again,
The figures on the steps beneath the balustrade
Now camera clicking tourists,
Seemed somehow almost invisible,
Passing ghost images,
Undisruptive of the watery echoes,
Play of light and shadow,
Balmy all-embracing air.
As if Fragonard, ourselves, these other interlopers,
Having been there briefly, had left without a trace,
Each transient human figure, face
Erased.

CATACOMB OF SAINT CALLIXTUS

. . . . Thy loving kindness and mercy shall follow me all the days of my life: and I will dwell in the house of the Lord forever.

Psalm 23

So as he whistles softly, imagine him,
Dust everywhere, in his nostrils, eyes and mouth.
Fulfilled, a believer, sure of his own redemption,
Sure also of his hands' skill
As he carves out yet another tier of niches,
Soft tufa stone ideal for this purpose
Yielding,
To lay down the mortal remains of those departed.

Whistles too, for who knows when,
But soon or late, at the Lord's absolute discretion,
He himself will lie in the bosom of this blessed congregation,
Awaiting the call to heaven.

So, as he whistles,
Envy him.

This faithful servant of his fate.
This fortunate.

SLIPPAGE

You can only live so long
Beside the people long departed.
Stoke up the fire,
Revive the conversation,
Breathe new life into the topicality of gossip,
Resume the posture of an acolyte,
Receive the wisdom of experience.

Try, you try so hard,
But, little by little as the days wear on,
New troubles and concerns,
Potentialities
Displace the originating grace
That set you on your way:
So guilt or gratitude is not enough.

The handclasp weakens, slips,
The upturned face falling away into eternity,
An expression that we dare not trace,
A trajectory we know is commonplace.

NOREEN CAMPBELL

It was only after training and serving as a nurse in Belfast's well-known Mater Hospital for over 40 years that I turned to creative writing, discovering in poetry and prose the opportunity to express so much of my rich and varied life.

My earliest inspiration, however, was found in Inch Island in County Donegal, my birthplace and childhood home. The hardships of rural life contrasted vividly with the beauty and tranquillity of a small island surrounded by Lough Swilly and the culture of Inch is woven into much of my writing today.

The pressures of raising a family in Belfast and becoming a widow in 1981, along with the commitment of working in the health service in a large city, only enhanced my experiences, developing further my desire to write. However it was only after retirement that I started to share my work - finding an outlet by joining Ruth Carr's BIFHE Poetry Publishing class in 2002.

GROWING UP

I played with my friends on the Mill Bay shore,
Built my castles, good as anyone.
Paddled, fished and ran agley
Content to be by the shore and free.

I climbed the pitching and jumped the rocks,
Fought my corner, good as anyone.
Laughed and cried, no inhibitions,
Content to be by the shore and free.

So life evolved and I fitfully grew
Into a woman, good as anyone.
Married and mothered and ran life's course,
Content to be needed, no wish to be free.

EVENING VISIT TO A GRAVEYARD

Evening falls, and soon the moon will rise to chart its silver wake
while I, my heart in shreds, dread the thought
that I will perish one day,
and wonder who will cherish my memory?
Then tears fall and I hear the distant call of a bird
and from its sweetness
I ask the Lord to hear my prayer,
"If to dust I must return,
wrap me in birdsong."

FAREWELL TO MARCELINE

Your long winter is over.
Bud forth in the Spring of Heaven.
Flower sweetly in your Eternal Summer.

SILENCE

The silence, deafening
midst all the noise,
uninvited came in.
No knock at the door.
It filled the room,
as stillborn you came from the womb.

GRIEF

I gazed at perfect whiteness,
Wood and flesh combined therein.
No flaw nor imperfection.
Tears blind,
As death in all its power is absolute.

COMATOSE

I lie here on grey ice.
The cold chills and I am helpless,
held firmly between life and death
in a winter's vice.

I look skywards to no man's land.
There is no light
and I am trapped
between the ghosts of dawn and the ghouls of night.

NIGHTMARE

Tall trees spread their branches from on high.
Their leaves crackle, like the cackle of a witch,
While from a nearby ditch, a little old man
With a spear in his hand cuts my flesh
And I scream with each slash.
Then I awake frigid with fright,
Another dream, another night.

IMPRISONED

In a prison cell where conflict stifles,
a woman on the verge rifles her pockets only to find
them empty,
and reads with the eyes of a blind man
a rare book she has written in her mind about her life.
A solitary life, an unopened letter
that no-one else can read.
She lives alone inside her head -
a dead battery.

DESERTION

Shattering shadows scatter across the floor,
and to the tune of the setting sun, as one they flit from
wall to door.
They twist and twirl, like boy and girl they prance, and
dance in an erotic stance.
Then suddenly swoop and are gone,
and I sit on my stoep, alone.

HOUSEWIFE

Just to be a housewife
is not a life.
Only an existence
with a persistence
of jobs to be done.

WINTER'S DREAM

'Twas the gloaming of a winter's evening,
and the cattle, softly lowing in the byre,
watched their breaths like vapour
rise higher and higher.
And in the pigsty next door,
the sow, contentedly grunting, suckled her litter,
their pink heads dunting for more and more.

'Twas the gloaming of a winter's evening,
and the woman, with tin can and spoon
beat a tattoo, long and steady, telling the men,
"Quitting time, tea is ready."
And now they come, man and dog,
towards home, the centre of their life,
from field and bog they wend
to mother, sister, wife.

'Tis the gloaming of a winter's evening,
and city lights and traffic streaming
sear the brain of an old man dreaming.

A LOSER

Mid March,
A cold night,
And a grey sky casts a grey light
On my world.

My world,
A cold place,
Where an empty bottle leaves an empty space
In my life.

Dreary night,
Ice cold rain,
Which chills the spirit but not the pain
Of a loser.

LIFE

Life's a drag.
This I heard from a hag who scratched her head and
smoked a fag,
and kept her money in an old canvas bag.

Life's sad.
This I heard from a lad who used a drug and always felt
bad,
and kept his money for fixes.

Life's jolly.
This I heard from a dolly who painted her face and said
"Oh Golly",
and kept her money in the bank.

Life's a curse.
This I heard from a nurse who sounded hoarse,
and kept her money in a black leather purse.

Life's great.
This I heard from my mate, who had little to eat, no
shoes on his feet
and no money.

NATURE

Burgeoning begonias, whites, pinks and reds,
tumble from terracotta pots.
An explosion of colour, they spill on Carrara marble,
defiant of its purity.
The message clear in the ruthless vigour –
"No storyteller in paint greater than me."

ODE TO A POTATO

You lie cradled in my hand,
Your creamy skin touching mine,
Sightless eyes wide open.

The hand in which you lie
Can show no mercy,
As hunger is pitiless.

LINDSAY HODGES

When thinking about how I came to write, I remembered coming home from school aged twelve having scored only 18% in a literature exam, 4% of which was for spelling my name correctly. Words were a struggle for years, with poetry always elusive. Only much later did the writing of the war poets and the work of existing and emerging Ulster poets take root in my imagination. The flowering of words, theirs and now my own, has graced my life.

I joined the Thursday group in September 2001 and have been fortunate enough to have work published in some magazines and publications since then. In March 2002, I read my first poems at the Crescent Arts Festival. 'Cook Yourself Calm' is included in this book as tribute to the vital role the Crescent continues to play in sharing creative arts with local people. In January 2003, I was awarded the Hennessy prize for Emerging Poetry for a long poem called 'Coming of Age', published in *The Sunday Tribune*. The first part is reproduced here, as the poem, a year in the writing, will always be close to my heart. 'A Song for my Father' was shortlisted for the Strokestown International Poetry Competition 2003.

I am now working towards my first collection and I would like to thank my family and my friends for all their support.

SURVIVAL INSTINCT

Planting bulbs is an act of courage -
a commitment to witness
the unveiling of petals,
a contract on both sides
profoundly rooted,
sealed by hands soil-deep,
gloves off.

Hope is cultivated
in corms for all seasons,
a cycle of life
as flaking husks of gladioli
fill the gap between
faithful crocus
and late-blooming tulips.

A prayer whispers into the loam,
offered on bended knee,
that both bulb and planter
will emerge unscathed
from hyacinth-dark months,
facing up to daylight -
surviving by instinct.

from **COMING OF AGE**

I – Maternity Ward

15 May 1981

They talked as if she wasn't there,
Platitudes offered like morphine -
It's for the best,
She can try again -
Words slipped into the vein,
Dulling the senses,
As if distress could be sutured,
As if only flesh was scarred.

She knew better, even then,
Her grief an open wound
Howling across the theatre,
Scenes unfolding in slow motion,
Through a gauze of pain
Opaque with deceit,
Pulsing like a heartbeat
That never was.

Her son. The child she never held.

ON RE-READING EDWARD THOMAS'
IN MEMORIAM

"The flowers left thick at nightfall in the wood
This Eastertide call into mind the men,
Now far from home, who, with their sweethearts, should
Have gathered them and will never do again."

Edward Thomas, Easter 1915

Amsterdam, Easter 2003

for Ruth

The flowers left thick at nightfall in the wood –
These bulb fields growing in a time of war –
Have trembled at the spoken word
At voices pleading until raw,

Until that moment of pre-emptive hush -
Uncertainty as speaking ceased,
They shuddered in the silence
The nightmare of uneasy peace.

Once blood was spilt for tulips –
Possession of one bulb enough to lose a life.
Now soil elsewhere gives cause enough,
Remains the currency of violence.

March hailstones carpet-bomb the petals
Denude their slender stems.
The circle of their stamens
Now lie like fallen diadems.

I wondered if there'd ever come a time
We'd have no need for flowers –
This year, trampled in the aftermath
There are none left to gather.

And in one corner of the field,
Like unarmed men and women,
Blind tulips turn their faces from the sun –
Will never bloom again.

LAST PRAYER OF A DINOSAUR

I dream of being traced –
misplaced for countless years
I have grown closer to the clay,
waiting for the century
when it's my turn to be unearthed –
an artefact caressed from sacred soil,
bones uncovered into light,
a brushing back sublimely intimate.

Not so deeply buried underground,
I am yearning to be found.

DESPITE THE WORLD ELSEWHERE

Somewhere –
despite the world elsewhere –
the flamingos are dancing,

a thousand ballroom couples
legs suspended prior to pirouette,
a courtship in cerise
where salt-plain shimmer
heat-haze glare
dazzle and confuse,

reality blurred
in whirl of oscillating beaks,
a festival of wings,
fantastic feet,

as if nothing else existed,
nothing mattered
only dance,
as if their pink and charcoal carnival
could revive a jaded earth,
a footsore people.

Somewhere,
the flamingos must keep dancing –
despite the world elsewhere.

FIRST IMPRESSIONS

Glasses off, I'm as blind as bats are reputed to be –
yet with visionary sightlessness,
I detect every second,
hear every word when it's whispered.

Sans contact lenses, outside is a blur, indefinable,
like walking through trees by Monet,
feeling paint on my face,
osmosis of colour through natural canvas.

Without foresight myopia's magical,
reflections improve without looking too close,
Hall of Mirrors distortion that isn't as bad
as expected, may even be better.

This is how I prefer it to be –
pushing my way through the earth like a mole,
paying closer attention to things that are missed
in the everyday world of the sighted.

Without focus, realism shrinks to a welcoming fog –
a cutting-edge culture blunted by distance –
a rarer existence,
but visibly more liveable.

RECONSTRUCTION

They chose me for the part
because I looked a little like her –
some echo in the high arch of a cheekbone
or the birthmark on our arms –
though her clothes are ones I'd never wear,
those shoes already causing blisters.

I'm asked to walk the route she took
on the day she disappeared,
but I don't know which path to take
when the road forks –
I have no instinct to go left or right
or comprehend where either ends.

I am a memory-jogger.
A substitute for what the people want,
and the disappointment in their eyes
the over-riding fear
that I am her and not her
is almost killing.

I have become a stranger to myself.
Even my name is lost to me
as I pad the streets by proxy
to some dreaded destination still unknown,
a walking ghost
unable to find her way back home.

FLOTSAM

for the unknown woman found drowned at Murlough Bay, 1928.

It seemed too easy to simply walk into the sea
weighed down by globes of granite
in the pockets of the dress her mother made.
Instead, not quite ready for her fate
she lay down by a rock pool,
the morning lapsing into afternoon, then evening
until her hair turned into carragheen –
a pelt of stippled seaweed –
skin hennaed by the sun,
her earrings wendletraps that caught the dying light
and spiralled like a fine Venetian tower.
She bore no rosemary for remembrance –
found only sandwort, campion, valerian for sleep,
fingers clutched around a mermaid's purse
as all around her limp-limbed starfish drowned in air –
the ocean came too late for them, too soon for her.

When it stole in, that tide of seven times salt,
she immersed herself in wave-cut sediment,
her outline made of shells in place of skeleton –
blue-veined limpet, mussel, razor, periwinkle, scallop –
the buried treasure of her body embedded in the stone
the hidden layers of a life unknown.

A SONG FOR MY FATHER

In the winter garden
a robin dances with my father,
their movements balanced
in synchronicity of spade and wing,
a ritual performance in a chill
that would lower any other man
in weather two months shy of spring.

I never knew which happened first –
the birdsong or his pipe –
but instinct makes both start at once,
the robin quick to understand
that sudden strike of match
is an opportunity for singing,
bird becoming master of the man.

Impressed behind the glass,
I watch my father rock his heels
beside the lupins - the way his body
used to stir itself delivering a speech –
and smile at how the habit lingers,
as, for once, a soloist outperforms him
from the branches of a copper beech.

COOK YOURSELF CALM

When my blood is reaching boiling point –
Another day slaving over a hot desk,
Grilling some hapless individual –
Only cooking calms my nerves,
Minus the TV chefs, or weighing to the measure.
I'm leisurely with cuisine,
But with anger so extreme I'm well past pasta
I ease my rage into a risotto,
Seeking solace with the onions,
Pouring out angst with a little olive oil –
Tuscan, last bottle from the market in Siena,
Where only terracotta tiles flamed red
And I was at peace in the piazza.
Spoon-deep in earnest concentration,
Stirring until steam no longer leaves my ears
I simmer to a standstill.
Wrath reducing with a sauce
Fortified by wine – for my health's sake –
I find a way to cook myself calm,
Dreaming of a place
Where all that grates is parmesan.

BLACKBIRD AT YOUR DOOR

Each time I pass your house
he is singing in the rowan,
gracing the same lithe branch
in and out of season,
liberating
that singular exquisite song –
and yet you always strike
the more compelling tone,
voice the sweeter note,
realise the more enduring way home.

BLUE BEYOND MIDNIGHT

There's no true definition of a mood –
no lines of demarcation -
so many shades of meaning
in a word,
but none that match
the hue of longing
more than blue,
deeper than an artist's palette,
as if I'd slit
the slender skin of water,
slipped under,
found the subtle tone of irises
reflected
in the sheen of dolphin,
painted language
wet with colour
on the ocean floor -
only for it not to hold,
tongued away
by shifting sand.
Swimming back towards sky
that's darker than the deep,
I resurface,
blue beyond midnight,
salt on my lips instead
of speech,
wondering what it is
that always draws me here -
and why
there is no turning back
to grey.

TOM HONEY

I was always interested in poetry and still remember poems learned at school and which had greatly impressed me. But of course the years have seen my interest develop according to the poets I encountered and 'discovering' a new poet is exhilarating.

As a primary teacher I always sought to interest my pupils in poetry, reading to them, encouraging memorisation, even drawing on them to compose their own poems. I have been attempting my own poems over many years now and, long retired, can devote more time to the task. As a slow worker, however, it can take me months to finish a poem. Some themes have been in my head for years and have not yet made transition to the page.

The following selection reflects my personal and creative interests, for I write about people – people close to me and people I observe. The natural world also fascinates me and I respond as best I can in poetry.

Tom Honey has had poems published in *Poetry Ireland* broadsheet, *The Belfast Telegraph, The Irish News, Omnibus* and *The Lonely Poets' Guide to Belfast*. He won first prize in both the *Poetry Ireland/Cooperation North* and the *BSA 'Year of the Family'* competitions and was awarded joint first in the Greenpeace/Fortnight competition.

SHINING ARMOUR

The compliment – for I sensed no guile –
turned my head a little.
"Thomas," she said and her smile,
resting on me like an accolade,
redeemed the cliché. "You're a knight
in shining armour!" So she repaid
the lift that saved her a long walk
in a downpour. Rain spears broke
against the windshield. Our talk
was of poetry and her next reading.

For days afterwards her compliment
nourished my thoughts, breeding
the sweetest notions of self-esteem.
I confess I liked the pose of knight,
finding a new gloss in an old dream.
Chivalry called, and oh the ache
to be seen as valorous!
Dragons or windmills I could take
or leave, but there was a deal more
out there needing the lance.

In steadier moments, alas, I knew the score.
Knightliness was out. Only the suit
of armour was mine. Who but me
had fashioned its parts from boot
to helmet. I'd clanked day after day
to school in it, wore my Sunday best
in it, let my voice go astray
in the depths of it. What chance now
to free myself of this carapace,
hear the real me, see the real face?

RAISINS

Sardis behind us, its remaining columns
holding only sky, we came upon
the vineyards and our bus slowed again.
Baskets full of winking grapes were passed
from hand to hand to the road's edge.
There, on the flattened margins, spread
over sheets of plastic and cotton, lay
dismembered bunches, a highway
of bronzing fruit losing its freshness
to the sun. "Raisins," shouted everyone.
And all the way to Izmir we could see
a harvest shrivelling, another being made.

In a stone jar she used to keep them
stored, I remember, high on a shelf
and in a wordless ritual she'd place
a small heap on my desk when I ploughed
Latin furrows or climbed Higher Maths.
Sweets, in those days of rationing
were absent friends. My books had grown
into a mountain unscalable for her
but she watched my slow ascent approvingly.
I didn't really want the raisins
but guessed she wanted me
to want them. My memory
is of munching through those study years
as if her store was inexhaustible.

IN MEMORY OF CYRIL MURRAY

Something of the darkness you'd lately
pulled yourself out from shadowed
your eyes that day, yet your wit,
still keen, punctured our best speeches.

Beneath our staff-room banter, though,
a sense of loss. Committed teacher
whom commitments drained, too late
we saw that we had not been

vigilant enough; now your retirement
and our rush of tributes, telling
you nothing you did not know
but never sought to advertise.

I phrased my wish for you in Irish,
I remember, to end my speech.
Go raibh blianta sona romhat –
may the years ahead be happy.

Just that; there were no intimations
that your future would be other
than we reckoned it. We pictured you
footloose in fragrant places around

Donegal, your easel in the heather,
your eye relishing the light
breaking through cloud round Errigal:
and you'd have music near, a tape

of Mozart maybe, delicate
in the mountain air –
unreal, unreal! All our goodwill
powerless to fend off terror,

your innocence no shield as killers
tore through your home one midnight,
mounted the stairs and found you
wide-eyed at your bedroom door.

REFLECTION

The mirror gave you back your tired smile.
We watched the nodded greeting as your words
came haltingly. The moving lips you saw
were reassuring so you talked some more.
We should have interrupted yet we kept
our distance, troubled by this new decline.
"I've asked her in for tea," you murmured then.
"Why won't she come?" We could not bear
your eyes' bewilderment but took your arm
and led you slowly to the open air
to listen to a blackbird somewhere near.
We covered every mirror from then on
but found no cover for our growing fear.

FIVE FINGER STRAND

How you must have loved moments
like these on the strand, under
the high dunes and the cliffs,
the sun, gold turning bronze,
lowering into Trabreaga Bay.

I look for detail your painter's eye
would have delighted in, like how
the sand, combed into undulations
by the tide, catches the honeyed
light; how scattered wrack flares,
reveals its amber core, everything
made gentler at this hour –
sea holly on the upper shore,
the marram crowding the dunes.

I come in late homage, friend.
You could be walking just ahead
so strongly do I feel your presence,
but the sand remains untracked.

And all those images of Inishowen
redeemed for you the dark of Belfast,
your brush bringing them home.
Tears come, thinking of that final image
you beheld, the stranger in a balaclava,
gun in his raised hand.

TINNITUS

Less a ringing than a low sibilance,
a slow puncture in the head, a sound
I've almost come to terms with, excepting
times like now when, trying out thoughts
in lines across a page, I resign myself
to this misted silence. If, in the noisy
flotsam of the day it seems withdrawn,
I need only settle down to think
or play at shaping verse to bring it
like a wreath of midges round my head
until I feel I'm eavesdropping on wear
and tear. Though there are mornings when
I seem to drown in torrents, mostly
day opens as it ends, in a long-drawn
sigh like fine sand falling and I pretend
indifference to the hour-glass in my head
endlessly spilling irrecoverable grains.

BLUEBELLS

We could have chosen better –
any of those blue-ceilinged mornings
May had brought, but now we climb
through overcast. Cavehill frets
in a drizzle, glum as the pewter Lough.
I turn, responding to your cry.
Gathered in drifts beneath the trees
we find the truant sky.

WEEKEND COTTAGE

i.m. Jim

Mildewed walls, sour sting of soot,
a range rust-blistered. In the grate
a jackdaw's scaffolding of twigs.
Little for us to celebrate.

But we gave our borrowed cottage
months of weekends; brought back the colour
to its cheeks; saw to the chimney's throat,
helped the sun heal the dank corners.

Jim painted on the staircase wall
The Seven Dwarfs in bright ascent.
The children took to them and made
Hi ho, hi ho, their bedtime chant.

Mornings saw them in fragrant fields
chasing the baler on its round.
Straw-pricked arms and skin aglow
charted their days lived far from town.

Lamplight; then a rush of stories,
patchy chronicles per child.
Plans were sleepily considered.
The dwarfs heard everything and smiled.

But winter's talons stripped the gold
of summer. Damp rooms, choked flue,
a privy comfortless and chill
undid us. Disenchantment grew.

The weekends died and jackdaws claimed
the smokeless chimney. Cobwebbed panes
told much. Once, after thieves had been,
I visited the derelict again.

Sad shell! But there by the staircase
the dwarfs still climb with undimmed cheer,
expectant faces seeking Snow White –
Gone. Gone many a long year.

COUNTRYMAN

No matter that he has been fifty years
away from cattle, barns, potato drills,
the cut of countryman, confirmed by a face
that maps the weathering of earlier times,
has never left him. City dweller, yes,
but not a city man. Look at him now,
perched on that bollard on the Antrim Road,
his pipe a seal on his contentedness
as if he'd spent the morning at the hay.

And that's how I remember Patrick
through distant summers – he and his brothers,
brows streaming, pitchforks glinting, and the stacks
multiplying in the stubbled field.

I touch the car horn, wave; he tilts his stick.
At once I see those clean-cut acres,
catch their fragrance still.

CONVERSION

For all the clustering whiteness
of his hair and meditative pose
in church last week, Cloot Connery
loomed greatly in my boyhood woes
when my ripe imagination cast him
as despoiling Dane. What terror
when he swept his guldering band
of yobs towards us, souring our summer
with their bin-lids and brush shafts
making thunder in our street. We ran,
our gang preferring any other day
for battle, choosing to defy
them from behind closed doors.
So tough was Cloot my timorous eye
saw muscles in the undulations
of his hair. Height and the loudest voice
confirmed for me his fearsomeness.
But time gives reason to rejoice.
I scanned that pious figure, so still,
monk-like in the long coat he wore,
and came to recognise that Cloot
had torched his long-boat years before.

SURVIVOR

It must have been a near thing
with a cat that left its wings
askew, and hanging so they seem
like blackbird hand-me-downs, the sheen
gone from the plumage. Survivor
now from seasons past, familiar
on my lawn, his unkempt look
wins favours though starlings loot
the bread I throw. That said, he knows
how to sell himself, for I note
at evening, time and again,
on that larch bough at my garden's end
his ragged silhouette appears
and well before the stars emerge, he stars.
Hedgerows ring with a backing choir
but it's his voice that I listen for.

NOTES FROM THE PAST

Dad's soprano resonated through family lore
so constantly I often tried to picture him
aged twelve in old St. Joseph's church before
the altar singing Adeste at Christmas Mass.

"Came from all around to hear him," aunts used to say,
their pride in recollection disregarding
the piety of those who came to pray,
buoyed by the joy of nativity.

The story had its villain, too – the choirmaster.
"Kept him singing too long. Should have rested
the voice before it broke. A disaster"
thought the aunts, seeing a talent squandered.

Once, for the four of us, from his old repertoire
Dad mined a hymn about a Green Hill Far Away
and took off in a strained falsetto, to restore,
I suppose, a remembered solo glory.

I was the eldest and it pains me still
that my unmanageable sniggers set the others off.
It was like targeting a bird, watching it fall
at our feet. Dad stopped mid-note. He didn't scold.

Just said, half-theatrically, half in pain,
"I'll never sing again." Mind you, he did
but we knew that day we'd heard his requiem
for what was long beyond recovery.

CATHERINE LESLIE

I began writing poetry a few years ago and have been part of two local writing groups for almost two years. A lot of my writing focuses on human relationships and emotions. I am also concerned about animal rights and try to express my views with humour, which has been described as 'astringent'!

I prefer to hand-write my poems and this is the first time they will have been set down in print.

I could say writing creatively has been a good decision, only not so much a decision, more of a spiritual imperative. Poetry feeds my spirit and it's always very hungry!

POEM

Read me in a whisper
Slip into my rhyme
Read me in a secret voice
A voice that's yours and mine
Slide into my rhythm
Suspending us in time.

Ingest, devour my metaphors
So very easily swallowed
They never fall on barren ground
Only ground that's hallowed
Soak my words in colour
Delight in their meaning
Relish the intensity
Always self-revealing.

Read into the spaces
Look behind the lines
Subject me to a deeper read
I'm all the art you'll ever need.

TRANQUILITY

In quietude beside the river
Rapt in its cool and watery ribbon
Following its intention
Flowing freely home.

Sense the spirit in the body
Flushing out the melancholy
Listen to the lispy whisper
Rolling over under ripples
Rising from the mother bed
Bringing forth a watershed.

EMPTINESS

Whatever has been is not so indelible;
whatever will be not always inevitable.
An insoluble riddle when you're caught in the middle
of nothing.

How can you miss the one you are with?
How can you miss someone you've not met?
Why do you search in a void?

How can you bear to think love is so finite?
Why do you care to deny it?
How can one space fill another?
What is it that happens
when the two come together?

And what of the places in between these wide spaces –

inaccessible, redundant or dead.

MAKE NO BONES ABOUT IT

The flesh boiled off your bone
with style.

Your smell, it owned the room
awhile.

Your shin, it was,
whenever that was,
divinely sawed
and easily dislodged.

An easy cow, not a queasy cow

Was a clean bone

No flesh clung

Not a bad cow

Certainly not a mad cow

Undistinguished

Anonymous.

COLOURS

Tuesday's child is full of grace,
A bright and silvery drop of dew
Seated on a golden lap,
Enshrined within a pinky hue

Gratification's creamy white
Feeling loved an orange light
Rage is black and on its own
Grey is sad and all alone.

Humility is liquid green
Humiliation can't be seen
Fiery red's a lump of pain
But tell me then,

What colour's shame?

A4

I ate your limp today
from the allotted
space on my plate,
with chips.
Imagine!
That fragile little
leg
supporting all that body muscle.
Ate
a lot of that on
Sunday.
Fried
your wings on
Monday,
were
Nuggets
on the
Tuesday.
Dog
had you on
Thursday.
A quite impressive
spread.
Yes,
it must be said
you go so far
when you're
dead.

ROMANCE

Romance.
Don't talk to me about
Romance.
Look! There's a man in the middle.
Typical. Talks eroticism.
It's a cataclysm.
Or some other *ism or asm.*

Romance.
Not another word.
It's clichéd and absurd.
Whisper sweet nothings.
Ha! See. Typical.
No substance.

HELP

How much more do you need
to read
you're
ugly, neurotic, selfish, psychotic
self-esteem is anorexic
thoughts perverse
relations toxic,
gobbling up pages
spewing out rages
ashamed of your greediness
hiding the neediness
scrubbing out feelings
making them clean things
pills didn't cure
only made you a whore
a chemical disaster
seeking happy ever after
from a horizontal hiding place.

AWAKE

Standing in the doorway.
Looking at the body.
Feeling other-worldly.

Thinking all she cannot do.
Wishing I did not have to.
Expectations crushing.

Distant from the body – Death.

Abstract from the other – Life.

TIME AND SPACE

Before the door opened, before
she was found, innocence
uncrushed, before
time was a lush, before
the old lust. After
the door closed –
not in her mind, dressed
in deceit after
the clock chimed. After
the seeds sewed, before
they were roots,
the space in between,
the shape that it took. After
resistance, when silence
was sacred, warm
as the womb when
life was stripped
naked.
Remains
in a room –
Tight
as a tomb.

STAR

And
I will
give you the
Star of morning
as you rest in your bed of clay
set the skylarks singing to mellow approaching day.
And from the lucent drapes of dawn
cascades of blessings tumble on you
and thoughts divine fall soft upon you
in little beads of rain.
And when the arms of night enfold and day begins
to sleep, the steadfast Star of Evening
is forever
yours
to keep.

DENIS O'SULLIVAN

When I retired a few years ago, from a long career in computing (well to tell the truth I am still not totally retired!), I decided to pursue a lifelong interest in writing in a practical way by joining one of BIFHE's Creative Writing classes. Even though I wanted especially to write short stories I soon found myself dabbling in poetry as well.

'The Migrants' and 'Professional Pride', both included here, are the results of my earliest experimental steps in what was to me a very unfamiliar form, but they were enough to get me interested and I now attend Ruth Carr's *Poetry Publishing* class as well!

I have been encouraged by early successes with a short story, 'The Blacksmith', published in *Ireland's Own* in October 2002 and a poem, 'Asbestosis', in *The Lonely Poets' Guide to Belfast,* published in 2002 by New Belfast Community Arts Initiative. 'Asbestosis' also appears in this anthology.

THE MIGRANTS

Autumn's leaves lie listless on the ground
their duty done for yet another year
while birds as if by seasonal command
prepare to make a journey that they fear
and gather in long rows and wait before
the scents of summer lingering in their minds
dispersed by icy wind from northern shore
will lure them to those distant warmer climes.
These native shores are rumbling with unease
shaping the rocks to roll beneath our shoes
with strata plaited deep in angry seas
in colours of such multivaried hues.
And rising high above the swelling ocean
the birds depart with barely a commotion.

ASBESTOSIS

Goliath straddles the once proud dock
Now empty but for scraps left
By the Koreans.
Titanic commemorated on celluloid,
No such glory for the scraps of men
Ravaged by the Rip Van Winkle dust
That slept for forty years.

A VIEW ACROSS BELFAST LOUGH

An Autumn morning;
Sun peeps above the eastern hills,
Cranes float on lingering mist
Screening reality from my sight
For just a moment.

Then Winter comes;
No light but man's
Marks the shore beyond the bay
Flashing a warning briefly red
For just a moment.

Spring changes all;
Soft colours paint the distant hills
Shivering in water sparkling bright
With all the joy of newborn day
For just a moment.

Summer's here;
Morning silver clothes the Lough
Warming the soul of every man
That lifts his eyes to look
For just a moment.

THE WATERWORKS REMEMBERED

The centre of our universe
It was our playground in those days
Where wary eye for ranger scanned
The banks of lakes that were our sea.

Beyond its boundaries, not far,
The whack of leather ball on boot
And bat, for cricket too was played,
And racquet twang for love or deuce.

Swans afloat with haughty ease
Their kingdom mapped with webbed power
While man-made sails with greater stir
Could only imitate their grace.

McArtt looked down with friendly eye
Across the waterworks' expanse
Protecting it from winter winds
That bore Siberia's icy breath.

So friendly then so ugly now
The progress of our modern age
Has made our fairyland a waste
Of needles, crap and plastic bags.

PROFESSIONAL PRIDE

I cherish the moment when I glide onto the stage
and the music begins.
Perish all thoughts of shame.
I cavort under the gaze of my ardent fans until I discover
a ladder in my tights. It makes me
madder than a hornet.
It may be erotic to some of my admirers
but for an exotic dancer, it is certain
to cause swearing later, not caring whether it is right
or wrong to make a song and dance about it.

PAPER DREAMS

Meeting at corners
Creases sharp as razor edge.
Bright layers, gently enfolding.
Flowers opening, petals like stars,
Birdwing beating, beaked head pointing.
Elephant ears flapping, pleated trunk trumpeting
Paper notes of triumph ascending, in a rainbow universe.

SPEAK NOT ILL

A quite outstanding man, you say
His like we seldom meet these days
A man of boundless energy
Involved in every charity
A prototype of piety
An icon of sobriety.
In business, selfless probity
Exemplary propriety
A family man in every way
We lay him here to rest today.
The man I knew was autocratic,
Bucolic, manic, vitriolic,
No good to say of lay or cleric
But then – this is his panegyric.

THINKING OF SOMETHING

I am thinking of something that no one but me could
possibly know.

It claws its way into my mind as I walk by the river
watching the rippling shadows
of clouds racing across the drowned sky.
It grabs my attention in a stranglehold
as I contemplate shivering
trees burrowing into the watery earth.
It calls to me in soft voices filled with
anticipation as birds drift lazily
in the blue sky shimmering beneath my feet.
It lulls my brain with persistent whispering
promising peace as shadowy fishes flit
across the river's weedy floor.

It makes me think of something that no one but me
could possibly know.

WAITING FOR THE RIGHT MOMENT

Good red wines improve with age.
Complex flavours of fruit
And chocolate, yes chocolate
Ripening to dense colours
Of blackcurrant and peppery plums.
Plummy I love.

Good white wines have shorter lives.
Pale straw to golden corn
Scents of vanilla, apricot, lime,
Creamy bouquet of gooseberry
Smooth as butterscotch.
Buttery I adore.

I can take no more of this.
Fetch the corkscrew.

FLICKERING CANDLE

The flickering candle breathes the dying air
Exhaling light that like an artist's brush
Paints images of love that make me blush
Remembering how much we still can care.
In younger days, when vigour was to spare
We savoured lovers' passion in its flush
With tender words, soft kisses, gentle touch
Making the fires of pleasure rise and flare.
Younger still, so fierce the furnace roared
Fuelled by hopeful look and loving glance
Falling as coals upon the glowing hearth
Fanning the ardour that in rapture soared
As if we might not get another chance,
To consummate our love upon this earth.

EULOGY FOR A FISHERMAN

Around the rim of his battered tweed hat
he wears his feathers
like a crown of thorns.
From dawn to dusk the lash,
applied with scarcely diminishing gusto,
stripes the skin of the lake
with gentle ripples.
At ease with nature,
the quiet of solitude lures the spirit as
gentle barb in silence
hooks the soul.
Deep thoughts, fed upon the silence,
sink to the stony bed
then upward fizz
in flagrant flight of glorious meditation.
The spreading ripples
wrap him up in peace
that is the core of self and self the core.

SIGNS OF LIFE

Coiled in a web of nods and beckonings,
pursed lips, smiling mouths
frustration stares from his sad eyes.

Wrapped in dead air unmoved by sibilants
he cries his mental prayer
for deliverance from the silent cave.

Seeing the flow of words he does not hear
he tries to trap the movement of their lips
without a rule to measure them against.

Help comes through hands that speak in signs,
a dictionary of hope that he can use
to launch ideas, thoughts into the world.

VIVIEN PATON

I am married, live in South Belfast and worked as a clinical physiotherapist in the health service for many years. I began to write two years ago following retirement. I focus on both poetry and short stories. I have had a poem published in *The Lonely Poets' Guide to Belfast,* and have printed a children's book to celebrate the birth of my grandson.

In poetry, I am interested in exploring human relationships, especially pivotal moments that can change the pattern or direction of a life. I also find inspiration in growing things, animals and the spiritual life.

HAIKU

I

The crazy woman
Smoking, ash falling unheeded
Onto her lapels.

II

Chimes on a windy night
Wake me from a dream, melting
Into the wax moon.

III

Chagall on the roof,
Violin, knee flexed, he dances,
Shiva in heaven.

SEPTEMBER

When morning touches piebald leaves
The sun weakens in sadness.
Signalling a closing down, an introversion
In plant and animal.

I saw you for the first time.

The shock of recognition
Pulled us together as iron filings to a magnet.

Intoxication, madness, they said.

Full-flood moment gone, the seasons changing
We drifted like flotsam in the equinoxal wind.

A third of a century later the memory returns
In the slanting September sun.

Outside my window, the willow weeps.

SUMMER EVENING

The last rays of the sun
Variegate the box hedge.
Blackbird sings in the oak.
Piercing, sweet.

Water is running behind the hedge.

Swallows chase each other in the shadows
Drifting on air currents
Like surfers on waves.
Lingering light paints their feathers
Mottled gold.

Through an open window
Mozart's music,
Delicate, perfectly harmonised
Crystalline sound.

Sound and light merge
For a moment
Then gone –
Shadows move forward.

BEACH IN WINTER

Savage sea lightens the sand
To a softer sheen.
The mountains lit from behind by a pale sun
Crouch like a black hunting beast,
Alert for flight or fight.

A small dog with feather-like tail
Moves with easy grace
From the fringing sea's edge
To the marram grass,
Growing tufted and stiff between the rocks.

A few stern figures march the beach,
Hunched against the wind's attack.

From where I sit on a chilled rock,
Face growing numb,
Extremities rebelling,

I am hypnotised by the power of the sea.

The ego shrinks to walnut size,
A floodgate opens, to surge through
And clear muddied waters.

I am shipwrecked on another shore,
A helpless child, beginning again.

POEMS FOR MY PARENTS

I - Easter Sunday

My mother died on Easter Sunday.
A vibrant sunshiny blustery Easter day,
Waking the daffodils and blowing winter away.
I missed her leaving by half an hour.
We missed each other all our lives.

II - In Life

In life my mother's spirit
Clenched, painful,
Deformed as the joints.
The ghost of her father never absent,
Forbidding her to love again.

Death releases her from a windowless room
To walk in a summer garden,
Laughing at squabbling sparrows,
Lifting flawless hands to catch magnolia petals.

III - November 11

On Remembrance Day my father died
When the old men were marching,
When the poppy petals were falling
He forgot about war.

Red petals, white petals.
Confetti for their wedding.

AUTUMN

Elderly people
Move slowly
Over slippery leaves
Sad with rust.

Winter narrows the sky
And turns the spirit
Inward.

NOT IN SERVICE

She leans from the train
Clasping his hands.
"Will they like me in the big house
Will I do?"

"You'll do, my love, you'll do."

A young man with untutored hands,
At home with beasts and barley,
Reaching a fork in the road.

The whistle blows.
He sees her eyes,
Lifts her from the train
Holds her as it pulls away.

Laughing, crying, they take the dog-cart
Home.

THE PIANIST

Eyes intense and dark
To luxuriate
In whirlpool depths.

Long white hands
Caress the piano.

You watch absorbed,
And move a smooth stone
Along your cheek-bone.

Music tangible
In sternum and solar-plexus
Reverberating on tympanum
Shudders to a close –
The pianist locks eyes with you.

Outside the circle of desire
The spectators shrink to invisibility.

PLAYING CHESS WITH FATHER

Deceitful bishops diagonal in their thinking,
Knights controlling frisky chargers,
Front-line soldier pawns
Falling on advance, as at Somme or Marne,
Castles patrolling the perimeter.
Hen-pecked king trying to please,
Shambling to and fro
While his queen holds her place, imperious,
Waiting for opportunity – to win.

My father's wasted face
Alert with attention,
The twin strands of concentration and competition
Holding us close,
Diminishing pain, fear of the passing place, remorse.

After his death, remembering
Unfinished sentences, silences, a façade of jocularity,
How he check-mated me,
Tearing down the barricades
In his final game.

SKYROS

First there was the great golden globe.
Intense, it sucked life from the sea
To inhabit the red earth.

Then the Greeks making a design of their world
With goddesses, heroes and wars.

Their demise a secret held by the rocks.
Left behind blood-stained swords and spears
For the rats to lick clean . . .

Skyros remains
An island in middle sea.

Pitiless sun over the baked land.
Winter storms
Turn the red soil into rivulets of rust.

Goats roam free over the hills.
Dust flecks hang in the shafts of light.

Silence, except for the hum of bees
In the ancient olive groves.

MAURA REA

I always wanted to be a nurse; nurses make a difference. Though I chose in the end to be a full time wife and mother, I have cared for people all my life in one way or another and made my impact on their lives through deeds not words.

After twenty-one years though, with nursing now too late in the day as a career, I started creative writing as something to do for myself and then as something wonderful to share with other people. Writing is now such a big part of my life I have found that through developing my work I have grown as a person. I have found a voice I never knew I had. Now there's nothing I like to do more than express it. I have discovered that words, as well as actions, speak loudest of all and often mean more.

If my words can create a smile, a sigh, a tear, laughter, if they say "you are not alone", if they give you a voice, if through my poems I can achieve any of these things, I will truly feel I have made a difference more than I could have hoped for.

WHISPERING HER NAME

I found him
the morning after
we'd buried mother

slumped in his chair
clutching
bits of paper

crumpled in the
weight of
stark black print

his cradled palm
heavy
upon a box

layered with
paper –
newspaper
cuttings

"A Tiny Miracle"

buried in a shoebox
his voice little more
than whispering

Isabella.

FAILING A MIRACLE

Abandoned by the
wayside, certain of
death
in the hope of
life
the price of being
born
a little empress.

MAGIC

To see it falling
and scream
it doesn't matter
it bites

prod with twigs
poke orange and black
wrap in rags
feel its' frosty bite.

To see it fallen
and scream
winter's magic.

AIR WALK

The wind
breathes

a heavy
sigh

cloudy blue
and green

sway as
one

fear
drips

I close
my eyes

to the
waves

thrashing
in the

unfathomable
distance

my hands
burning

I inch salts
of solidness

paving
the firmament

my heart
pounding.

NO ONE CARES

In her stupor
she reaches
the bottle
empty
I make coffee
distancing
her raves
her words
ice my spine
I race the stairs
catch her wrist
force her hand
moist with tears
I settle her
in my father's
absence

clenched in my fist
an endless lullaby
her words aching
I wonder.

FIREWORKS DISPLAY

Mushroom clouds
fuelled with rage
lighting the sky.

His mother
his father
his arms
gone.

Their hands blistered
her father
her mother
peeling her burning flesh.

Without water
without power
without aid.

Fireworks display
the human cost.

PLAY ON WORDS

Power
control
domination
mastery
supremacy

greed
desire
gluttony
selfishness

agendas
concealed
disguised
shrouded
veiled

reasons
real or imaginary
actual or invented
conceived or contrived
fabricated or formulated

behind every war
there is a reason.

BROTHERLY LOVE

I don't want to
love him
but mummy says
I have to
and my teacher
says God says
I have to

I don't want to
love him
I have to.

PAIN NEEDS NO BATTLE

To my room he'd come
in the night
shadowed in the
dreams of mother's stupor
he'd play
I'd get hurt
to cry
disturbed mother's dreams
pain needs no battle.

In the pulse of night
he'd play
cradled in his strength
I hurt
while mother slept.

DEPTH HAS NO DIMENSION

The sky
ebony, starless
the clouds
icy grey
the moon
full, staring

nothing moves
nothing stills
nothing echoes
not sound
not silence
not time

depth has no dimension

everything
the wood
the stream
the girl
clinging to nakedness

unreal.

HE LOVES BECKY NOW

I hear his footsteps
passing
in their stillness
I know

silent
beneath the covers
I hide
pained in my bleeding
knowing

his passing footsteps
the long stillness
he doesn't love me
I have become a woman

he loves Becky now
I know.

WHITE COLLAR

Suited in black he
strolls the corridors
of his domain

our father
respected
white collar

behind closed doors
removing his collar
cloaked in black
he bullies.

FORBIDDEN FRUIT

A coat of black
shelters the beast
lurking within
hunger his driver

selecting prey of
pure tenderness
he thrives
in the garden of innocence
feasting
slowly savouring
the delights of forbidden fruit

satisfied he retreats
donning his coat of black
sated
until his next banquet.

MANUAL LABOUR

I don't do
buttons and bows

frills and fuss
not my style

less is more
more is

too much effort.

WORKER OF MIRACLES

i have turned
water into wine
stretched loaves and fishes
moved mountains
healed the sick
given sight to the blind
hearing to the deaf
all in one day

i am not
God
but I am
the next best thing
a woman.

PAT TAYLOR

I write mainly about my country childhood – its beauty and also its hidden violence. I was born in Belfast in 1932, left the city at the age of nine, to return again at nineteen. My first poem was written about my husband after his death in 1984. But it wasn't until three years ago, when attending the Writers' Group at Queens, that I began to put together a book of poems for my family, illustrating them with old photographs.

I now also attend the BIFHE Thursday class, 'Publishing Poetry', and have had work published in *The Lonely Poets' Guide to Belfast, Alchemy Poetry and Prose (an anthology produced by the Creative Writers' Network), Gown, The Honest Ulsterman* and also on a glass sculpture as part of the New Belfast Community Arts Initiative.

I would like to thank my son, Ross, for all his patient help on the computer and for his faith in me.

FULL OF NONSENSE

Learmount Castle 1943

A bank of rhododendrons
sloped steeply to the river.
Above, Learmount
reared against the sky.
Gargoyles snarled at us
and from the portico
speared dragons glared
across the woods.

There were no private moments
at boarding school,
so I'd excuse myself from class
and dashing up the servants' stairs
would pace the main landing,
imaginary fan clicking and rippling.

Reaching the grand staircase
I'd sweep back my long hair
and head high, would descend,
one hand languidly trailing mahogany,
the other raising the hem
of my flowing gown.

Stepping delicately across
checkerboard marble
I'd pause graciously,
as the Prince bowed low.

Too often I'd lose all sense of time
and only clanging brass
would return me to reality
of gym slip, ink-stained fingers
and the cold spaces
between stockings and interlock knickers.

AS SOON AS SAID
1937

On the mantelpiece
sepia tinted ghosts:
my father's friends
'still wet behind the ears'
mowed down
in the Somme's red mud –
and round-eyed cousins,
'My darling buds', Gran called them.
Like the greenhorn soldiers
no inkling of what lay in wait.

I gazed at them each day,
mourned their lives unlived
feared to have tomorrow
savagely snatched away.
Sometimes I'd look in the mirror
and say, "This is *me*,
I am *here*, this is *now*."
But 'now' was always gone
as soon as said.

RUINED

1937

Logs blazed and fissled
and the velvet throat inhaled
exploding stars.
With heated cheeks I sat cross-legged
at Father's tartan feet.
Our rug was reseda green
and thick, hand-knotted by Mother;
she was making another,
measuring and cutting
against a grooved rule.

A standard lamp with long silk fringe
encircled us in amber light,
cast moving pictures on the wall;
rabbits and birds, Father showed me how.
With pearl-trimmed knife
he peeled an apple
all in one wiggley spiral.
As it dropped the fire spat
and showed me a snake.

Then Mother noticed my new doll
had been given a bob,
like the one I'd got on Friday,
'Smarter than ringlets', I was told,
but she cried, "*Ruined!*"
and held me back while it burned.
The black throat roared along with mine.

JUST AS IT WAS

Claudy Co. Derry 1941.

The sun slanted through
the partly-open gateway
of the old walled-in garden,
an oblique bright rectangle
on the rough stone wall beyond.
With the rattley push-mower
my father sheared
our patch of daisied grass.
By the sun-blistered scullery door
my mother paused,
arms floured to the elbows
and wearing a bleached sack-apron.
She watched as I wheeled our cat
in the old Tansad.

Suddenly still, I looked, listened,
breathing heady scent
of yellow Honeysuckle-azalea
and warm damp new-mown grass;
sensing a need to remember
that moment, just as it was.

BY THE RIVER

Claudy 1942.

Lying beside the slow Faughan,
I breathe pungent scent
of warm damp earth.
Dragonflies swoop
above the amber flow.
Fish are hunting too,
there goes the *plump* plop
of a salmon re-entering water
and from a far field, like an echo
the lazy note of ball on willow.

Drifting waist deep
in meadow grasses,
I watch bees fumble busily,
their weight dipping the blooms.
Butterflies rise before me
colours flashing in the sun –
I hear, but do not see
a rabbit drum his warning code.
Entering the cool Plantin
I drink from a spring
that has already spoiled me
for any other water.

ACCUMULATED QUARTS
1943

Stone-floored, the waiting room,
grand for muck-caked boots
and projectile tobacco juice
that missed the spittoon (mostly
their aim was just astounding.)
Through sickly-sweetish pipe-fug
I saw each seasoned farmer
a bottle jutting from his pocket.
Some swathed in newsprint,
those without gleamed amber,
each a *quart* of sample for the doctor.

One old man nursed two,
perhaps delivering for the missus.
By the look of things,
wives had no time to run to doctors.
Spoiled by city comforts I sat stiffly,
skirts safely gathered in,
thought myself among tramps;
didn't recognise 'moneyed men'
right under my nose.

RESIDUE

Funny some of the things
tucked away in your wallet.
A faded picture, taken
when I was just sixteen,
the Catholic 'keep me safe'
and you a 'Right Footed' cop!
An ancient ticket
for a Nashville show.

The good things went
quite some time ago.
I gave our eldest
your heavy fishing coat,
the Omega watch,
a splendid evening suit.

Your sister simply
chose a single tie,
but I sent a locket
with a twist of hair inside;
cut while you lay
in the sinister polished box.

I'll keep these old cords.
Do you remember me
teasing in the car?
I stroked your knee and swore
velvet turned me on.
You pretended panic, said,
"People on the bus will see!"
How we laughed, two months ago.

ON THE BRINK

Black-green against fire-opal,
birch leaves pattern the evening sky,
tremble in still air.
Deep water reflects the tilted image
and mirrors a drowned tree.
Roots are bared by the eroding flow,
bleached by August's sun;
soon fish will flirt
among these summer leaves.

LITTLE SHAREEM

Afghanistan, 2001.

Better three thousand dead
and not one vengeful finger raised
to add you to that number.

Above the veil
your mother's eyes lament.
I am invaded by the pain.

Two years wise,
weight two bags of sugar;
there are no crumbs for you,
no blanket but the snow.

RETURN TO LEARMOUNT
1998

One of the dragons
is missing from the portico
and the eyes of the Castle
are blanked by hardboard.
Vandals have bludgeoned a hole
through the breeze-blocked doorway.

Anna won't entertain it.
She wrings her hands,
says tramps or worse
might be lurking
and she's going back
to sit in the car,
with all the doors locked.

But neither fear nor age
can curb me,
I wriggle through the gap.
Such a stench of decay.
My torch shows the Adam ceiling
with its clusters of oak leaves.

Vast dark rooms
yawn on each side,
but I am stilled
on black and white marble,
fearing a plunge
to the cellars below.

Lost in the shadows
I sense the children
we had been.
I listen for the tap and scuffle
of many indoor shoes
on polished wood.

Fallen plaster; rubble; rubbish.
At last some light.
A grimy jewelled glow
arching above the stairway.
We sang carols here,
six little girls to each rise
stained glass behind us.

Anna, still outside,
wails through the gap,
her banshee warnings company.
The mahogany treads seem sound.
Up, up and around I go.
My dorm.
A brass 2 still on the door.

Water has run down the walls
and a decomposing floor sags.
Lit by my unsteady beam
clumps of dark fungi quiver and rear.
"Buildings are like people," I think,
"better remembered as they were."

CLINGING

For a while when I opened the wardrobe
I would breathe the remembered scent,
clean-soaped skin, Old Spice, tobacco.
Sometimes I'd creep inside and closing the door
would savour you all around me,
pretending your cheek against mine
and I cradled and safe in your arms.

The scent is all gone now, the clothes musty.
Inside your shoes my hands find
the shape of your feet, deeply imprinted.

There is a corner of this room
I still can't bring myself to clean completely
where you would tap and blow the shaver clear;
I used to watch with silent disapproval
but now I know in the dust
particles of you remain.

AND SO ON

Do not be sad.
Rather, think of me
as multiplied
and multiplying;
in you and yours
and theirs.